ICEBERGS

IN

MORECAMBE BAY

Also by Tony Turner

Some I Did Earlier (TWM Publishing, 1996)

Reading The Signs (Cherrycroft Press, 1998)

Where Was I? (Cherrycroft Press, 2000)

Belief in Something Better (Cherrycroft Press, 2003)

How Far Away Australia Is (Cherrycroft Press, 2005)

Oxford, 1953-57 (Cherrycroft Press, 2007)

Dreams and Sudden Dangers (Cherrycroft Press, 2009)

TONY TURNER was born in Rabaul, New Guinea, in 1933 and grew up there and in Hong Kong, Manila, Sydney, Nottingham, Sheffield, Kingston-on-Thames and Ealing. He was educated at Cranbrook School (Sydney), Allhallows School (Devon) and Keble College (Oxford). Apart from two years at Their Majesties' pleasure in the Royal Engineers, he spent his official working life in ICI as an industrial chemist. He lives in Cookham, Berkshire and has a wife, two sons and a daughter, six grandchildren and not enough time.

He started to write poems during his Devon schooldays and continued to write intermittently while earning a living and bringing up a family. Theoretically retiring in 1990, he has been writing regularly ever since. His poems have been published widely in poetry magazines and anthologies and he has six previous collections: *Some I Did Earlier* (1996), *Reading The Signs* (1998), *Where Was I?* (2000), *Belief In Something Better* (2003), *How Far Away Australia Is* (2005), *Dreams and Sudden Dangers* (2009), in addition to the autobiographical poem sequence, *Oxford 1953-57* (2007)

He enjoys sharing poetry with others in Metroland and Temys Poets and giving readings, which he has done in venues all over the south from Hitchin to Penzance.

Tony Turner

ICEBERGS

IN

MORECAMBE BAY

Best wishes,

Tony Turner

1/12/'12

Published in the UK by

Cherrycroft Press
Popes Lane
Cookham Dean
Berks
SL6 9NY

British Library cataloguing in Publication Data. A catalogue record for this book is available from the British Library.

ISBN 978-0-9572030-0-6

ACKNOWLEDGEMENTS

Thanks to Frances Wilson for editorial advice concerning this and all my other collections.

Thanks also to the editors of the following periodicals in whose pages some of these poems first appeared:

Assent, The Frogmore Papers, HRGB SE Region News, The Interpreter's House, The Journal, Pennine Platform, Rhyme & Reason, South and *Weyfarers.*

Printed and bound by CPI Group (UK) Ltd, Croydon, CR0 4YY

For my scattered family and all my friends

CONTENTS

THE GOOD LIFE

MONEY-GO-ROUND

You all start equal.
You throw your hat in the ring,
put your boot on the highway, set off
with your dog and go. At first
you get chances, but do you spend
wisely, take the opportunities you get?
Do you get too greedy, spend too fast,
have bad luck? You land in trouble.
Can you keep out of gaol?

You have a bad run, are mortgaged to the hilt
but still can't pay your bills. You try to borrow
without security. Some want to help you
keep going, others only want to win.
Your ego's bruised and you've lost
interest. It's all been dragging on too long,
round and round, you're bored.
You get up and walk away. The winners
play on, count their assets, see who's got
the biggest pile, determined to get a result.

SOMETHING MISSING

"Devotion is not a popular commodity in business today...". David St John Thomas, Writers News, October1999.

What we need is flexibility
and professionalism:
the ability to follow
management guidelines and policies
however often they change.
We want you to welcome new initiatives
by getting on with them,
even if they don't
grab you. And we want you to work
anywhere we choose
to move you to. Flexibility.

But most of all we want you
to go without wingeing
when we decide
we don't need you any more.

Of course you are working for number one
and may decide to take a job
elsewhere at any time.
We don't rate experience;
if we really need it
we'll buy it back again.
What we need are
bright young people.

Confused? What you must understand
is this: we don't make products,
we make money. If we're short of it
we may need to sell
part of the business
and, of course, the people with it.
We can't be responsible
for what new owners do.

How to keep enthusiastic
in such a climate?
Well, you don’t.
We don’t want any of that
childish amateurism here.
Just do the job professionally.
By the book. Thoroughly. Yes,
working all hours, if necessary.
We will watch your performance
and reflect it
in your performance-related pay.

IT'S NICE TO BE WANTED

"*all the funny papers lie and fly around the place*", Oscar Hammerstein II, *Flower Drum Song*.

I write a weekly article
For a colour supplement
It's hard to think of fresh ideas
that grab attention, pay the rent.

There's really only one thing harder
When working for a Sunday rag:
Next day to see your work discarded
And still inside its plastic bag.

HOSPITAL CLEANER WANTED

Job Centre, Thetford, Norfolk, Jan 2010

You've advertised for *reliable*
and *hardworking* people.

Don't you see that what you've done
infringes human rights of some

lazy, unreliable folks?
Hopefully this is one of your jokes.

Please change your tone and ask
for anyone who'll do this task.

THE GOOD LIFE

"… we had the feeling there were no real people in this kind of life – just actors playing the role of being happy." *Karl Rabeder*

How many suits can you wear at a time?
How many cars can you drive?
How many beautiful wives does it take
To make a man feel he's alive?

I've got where I've always wanted to be
With the days of poverty gone
Yet with piles and piles of money to spend
What can I spend it on?

Larger homes, influential friends
And very exotic meals?
A private jet, the latest clothes
And cars with gold-plated wheels?

And holidays spent with other rich folk
In very exclusive places
Enjoying the best that the world can give
All wearing their happy faces

And wondering if this is what it's about
And which of these friends are true
Or are they all actors just playing a role
While searching for something new?

And am I an actor playing a part
Alone when the music stops?
Am I only content while the cheering lasts
But sad when the curtain drops?

How many suits can you wear at a time?
How many cars can you drive?
How many beautiful wives does it take
To make a man feel he's alive?

VIRTUALITY

Hackers come in the night
steal the virtual money from your bank
spend it
on the other side of the world
before you wake
with people who then
spend it again
before you know it has gone
and so on
and leave behind a virus which
scrambles your bank's computer
and your own
so you can never know
never show
the money
once was yours –
or ever existed.

DREAM TEAMS

There were three teams playing
in this dangerous game
on a large, barren pitch with boundaries.
Only two sides wore coloured kit;
the third looked like the spectators
who roamed over the pitch at will,
coming and going, getting in harm's way,
crossing the boundary into areas
forbidden to the visitors.
Action was unpredictable:
slow-moving, then suddenly explosive.
There seemed to be no rules
about the number of players;
substitutions occurred frequently,
which was just as well
as injuries were numerous
and often fatal. Although
there were no goals,
from time to time players scored,
which was strange,
as there was no referee or scorer,
though the visitors thought
they were in charge
and the President of the home side
pretended he was. "How long,"
I asked as I dreamed,
"does this go on?" But no one
seemed to know, though
the visitors assumed they could stop
whenever they wanted.

FLIGHT

Cabin doors to automatic!
and I panic. What am I doing
on this aircraft? I was only
seeing my friend, checking
his travel arrangements,
not going anywhere myself
and now I'm bound
for Buenos Aires and I've
no papers, no luggage,
no seat, no Spanish,
no hope of leaving this plane
even though we're still
on the ground and no one knows
who cares where I am.
Of course you can't get off.
Fasten your seat belt! shouts
the angry stewardess
as the wheels start to spin
and I know it's imperative
I go to the toilet, now.

MEDIA SCHOOL

'Now pay attention, Lesson Two :
Conducting a Public Interview.
Remember this, it's good advice,
Nothing is learnt by being nice.
Practice at length the angry tone
So sharp it cuts them to the bone,
Then let the accusations fly
And interrupt when they reply.

The point is this : we do not care
Who did what to whom and where.
We do not wish to understand
Why things did not go as they planned.
Complex ideas just don't belong,
The aim's to put them in the wrong.
To get the facts is not the game
We must know where to put the blame.

There are some useful words to learn
That you can use at every turn
"Why didn't" gets them quite defensive
"Why won't", "why can't", the list's extensive,
"Blunder" "farce" "mistake" "disaster"
You must ensure that you're the master.
Precede your view with "People say..."
And don't use "I", that's not the way.

If you can learn all you are taught
And do it well without a thought
And practice hard for year on year
Until your tone is most severe
Imagine the prize that will be yours
The flustered victim, desperate pause,
The weak evasion, half-admission,
The fault is theirs without remission!

In spite of all you've learnt to do
There's just a chance their point of view
May still be heard. Oh moment dire!
They may keep cool despite your fire,
They may reply in accents calming
With news that's really not alarming,
They may use facts, oh dear, oh dear,
Or, even worse, use logic clear.

Now that's a crisis! Time to use
Our most effective special ruse
Just interrupt them in their prime,
Say, "Sorry, we've run out of time!" '

PRESSING CONCERNS

Our media are a disgrace
They create a climate that's bleak,
They are always in somebody's face
With blame or attack.

Opinion's presented as fact
And privacy is not respected,
Good news is pushed to the back
When wrong-doing's suspected.

Good news, they say, doesn't sell:
A scare's what gets our attention,
But people want good news as well
And want more than a mention.

GRUMPY OLD MAN?

When parents feed their children fat in truckloads
And let them spend all day in front of screens
When gambling is encouraged as a "business"
And stoned is all some youngsters want to be

When it's bad to be a Christian in this country
And all right to be a scrounger claiming dole
When killers can be given petty sentences
And bad men can't be sent back to their homes

When more people manage health than there are doctors
And researchers tell us what we've always known
When pensions cost us more than workers' earnings
And bankers bring our fortunes crashing down

When our media cannot tell us any good news
And forever seek to trap and then to blame
Don't tell me that there is no cause to worry
The future's bright and all will be OK.

SUMMER IN THE CITY

Hot.
People swelter in tube trains,
laze in parks.
Young women
display their bodies
because it is so hot,
but also because
they celebrate their fugitive beauty
and their freedom to do so.

And indeed they are beautiful:
there is so much beauty,
so fresh and lively and full of joy
that it must be both a pleasure and a torment
for the young men around them,
driving them to find
their own, their special ones
quickly, before the summer ends
or sends their young bodies mad
or winter brings some respite.

A 21ST CENTURY RHYME

The washing's wet, out it must go,
I'll hang it in the sun to blow
And as I do I'll get a tan
Then I'll need a cancer scan.

The dinner's cooked, the roast smells fine
I'll wash it down with a glass of wine.
The cheesecake is designed to please
It's loaded up with calories.

I think I'll go and get fresh air
The paper says the quality's fair
The grass is long, the air is dry
The pollen count is getting high.

It's time for bed, I'll douse the lights
I share my mattress with dust mites
My pillowed head's on feathers deep
I am not sure they're good for sleep.

The music's beat is out of time
I cannot make my poems rhyme
The world and I are not in tune
I think I'm going pretty shortly.

COUNTRY LIFE

A solitary horse grazes the fenced grass
waiting for her next rider, looks up to see
a red kite soaring, floating over far fields
searching for the next elusive meal
and looking down as he passes
at a multitude of turkeys
unaware how short their lives are to be
stuffing their gullets with food
they make no effort to find or get.
As dusk falls, they are herded
into fox-proof cages to sleep soundly
while the vixen passing by can only dream
of a turkey take-away, but must search on
for a rabbit, sleeping bird or even a vole
to feed her hungry family. A man and dog
come by taking the evening air,
the dog running unfettered like the fox
free to follow a hundred scents
for the sheer pleasure of it,
but needing the walk because she is plump
before she is locked in to dream the night away
in front of a warm hearth,
while the man wonders whether
he will have to sell his horse
or how he will pay for the family Christmas
now that he has lost his job again.

VIEWS

EMMIE'S BRIDGE ON COOKHAM MOOR

Once seven bridges were required
to let wheeled traffic cross
the waterlogged or flooded moor.

Since 1929, there's just this one:
three soft brick arches capped with stone,
forty yards of metalled roadway,
three nooks each side for walkers
to let carts through.

The floods of 1928 swept away
the previous bridge.
A year later, Emmie Balfour Allan
gave thanks for many happy years in Cookham
with this remarkable gift:
for the love of the place.

The main road ignored it
passed to one side over a culvert,
as if this bridge was just a path over the Fleet
and swans building their nests
among the overhanging willows.
But when moor floods came again
traffic was glad to use it,
as the old causeway lifted
its one-way-at-a-time transport
over bridge and waters.

Now some believe flood relief
has changed all that –
it's cheaper not to keep it in repair.
The causeway's barred
by padlocked metal gates.

GREEN

March shakes us from our winter stupor
with shouts of yellow, defying us to sleep on,
but April, by stealth, suddenly overwhelms us
with GREEN. We are drowned in green
as if no other colour existed, overpowered
by its everywhereness and its newness:
the glowing shock of philadelphus coronarius aureus,
the crinkly salad-fresh leaves of witch hazel
the glazed green graspers of bryony,
the scalloped shells of new beech leaves
tasting the air. Hedgerows are alive with it,
tall towers suddenly display it, branches of it
over-arch the lanes making a green heaven.
Buds burst with vigour, making the most of this
Spring Offensive, before summer's deadening rays
dry, darken, dull, de-activate,
turn it from frisky-gambolling-lamb vigour
to staid summer-matron-of-the-earth green,
welcome still, but its ability to startle and enliven
gone for another year.

RETURN TO KING'S COPPICE FARM, MAY 2011

This was and is a farm field.
Wheat, rape, barley are all gone
like the cherries before them.
The footpath has widened to allow
visiting vehicles along a dusty road
fenced in by shiny wires on posts.
Notices on either side warn BEWARE
the wire's electrified. And what's fenced in?
Giant metal skeletons standing on bare earth
scraped clean. Nothing moves.
As if you've suddenly blundered
on some ruined airfield from the last World War,
or starting gates for giant robot races.

It's still a farm, but modern farming
can't afford to clothe this valley anymore
with restful green or even vivid yellow.
These are the fallow months before the farm
bustles again in late July, like a holiday camp
for birds, bursts with the noise
of fattening food gobbled from plastic pipes
and metal troughs, as turkeys in their hundreds
range the field freely within their pens.

Then, as suddenly as festive decorations rise
and houses hum with merry-making,
all goes silent here again,
save for the bulldozers, the scrapers-up,
restoring the land
for the empty months that lie ahead.

ON THE SOMERSET LEVELS

They came from all directions
but mainly from the east,
not all together, but in squadrons
each numbering hundreds
or maybe thousands, uncountable
as they came on and on
while the sky darkened
and the sun slowly disappeared in the west,
all making for the same destination
driven by some master plan
of unfathomable complexity
requiring them, at the end,
to merge and swirl
to stretch their skein,
then roll their ball,
a million moving dots
in aerial ballet
against the last light of day
and ending with a flourish:
a dying fall
into the thickening night
below.

EDGES

1. Lyme Regis

We're walking from our hotel
down the cracked path, edge slipping away,
through Jane Austen's garden
past houses boarded up because
they might collapse and be a danger
along Marine Parade. Across the bay
grey, greasy blue lias slides
to the shore, the past catching up with us
deposited all along the beach.
Golden Cap and Cain's Folly are unmoved.

2. On Golden Cap

The camera must be used: Seatown
to the left, Charmouth to the right,
sun glamourising chlorophyll
in farmers' fields, highlighting cows,
barns, hedgerows, streams,
but I'm warned
"Don't go too near the edge."
There's a man with a dog
who collects stones in her mouth
brings one for you to throw
nudges your foot until you do.
The man recalls the story of another dog
who chased a ball towards the edge
which fell shear away.

3. <u>Barton-on-Sea</u>

A house on the front, a view to the Needles.
People walk dogs on the grass strip
between it and the sea. There's a path
to the beach below, notices warn
of danger. Looking up, you see
where a garden slipped away. Roses,
honey-suckle, lupins adorn the cliff face.
On the beach, huge boulders brought from Portland
pile in defiance. But
the sea's not the problem.
It's water inland,
the cliff's peculiar geology.
They've told the residents
that nothing can be done.

VIEWS

I wish that I'd once strode on Striding Edge
Or walked on Haystacks to admire the scene
Or stood aloft on Pavey Ark's sharp ridge
Or skirted death by Wasdale's slippery Screes.

I didn't when I could: I never will
And views that I once saw I'll see no more.
I will not roam the snow-capped High Street fells
So must admire them from the valley floor.

And yet, how blessed am I that now and then
I am surrounded by these Lakeland views
And find again, again and yet again
That what the ancient psalmist wrote is true.*

* "I will lift up mine eyes to the hills: from whence cometh my help." *Psalm 121, King James I bible.*

ICEBERGS IN MORECAMBE BAY

the Kent Estuary frozen over
after weeks sub-zero.
Crowds gather at Sandside and Arnside
to witness the miracle.

A lone canoeist
threads his red canoe between the floes
looking for the north-west passage.

On shore
ice crystals grow on crystals
sprout from grass tufts
smother boulders, sheath railings
like a school chemistry experiment
gone out of control.

At the water's edge, broken sheets of pack ice
clamber over each other,
lie there like beached flatfish
or smashed crockery.

While Morecambe Bay prepares to take
the red-hot ingot of the sun
and quench it's fire, mist spreads
its soothing balm over the shattered landscape

and a lone photographer
trusting his Nikon and his tripod to the ice's edge
records it all for absent disbelievers.

IN GLENCOE

Clouds expunge the mountain tops
lour over the treacherous pass
threaten our safety.
Then rain scours the hillsides,
veils of it
hanging across the glen of sorrows,
slow, windblown undulations
concealing this wild beauty
like a bride.
Cataracts shower over rocks
scrubbing stone ledges,
atomising into mist
which floats across sad cliff faces
where sheep and ghosts share shelter.
Water tumbles down gorge sides
like stairs weeping,
the road a long, curving gutter
flooded with grief.

The order to massacre the MacDonalds was given by Sir John Dalrymple, later first Earl of Stair, 1692.

ST KILDA

Beyond the Outer Hebrides
ravaged by Atlantic storms
six small islands: history in grass and stones
home to birds and sheep
deserted roofless houses
a village without people.

Yet people clung to these rocks
five thousand years
owed allegiance to the McLeod of Dunvegan
in 1667; grew barley, oats
caught and ate seabirds
kept sheep and cattle
were self-sufficient.

Low-built houses, cemented with dry earth
roofed with turf, warmed by cows in winter
gave way to Victorian roofing,
a second room, visitors in yachts,
then tourists, showing them what they lacked.
Forty-two left for Australia, settled in Melbourne
gave their islands' name to part of it.
Others stuck it out: hunger, 'flu, war,
the isolation after, gave up in 1930.

Sheep graze sheltered by cemetery walls.
The turf-topped cleits store
nothing. Mist shrouds the hills
obscures the lonely jetty
hides ghosts. From Boreray
the gannets and the cackling fulmars
proclaim their guttural victory.

ARTS & SCIENCES

BOOKS

Publishers fear we'll shy
at their prices and not buy
unless they're heavy. Literature sold
by the pound. Impossible to hold
in a hand. Bulky to lug around.
Shelf-eaters. Is the art lost —
page-packed volumes light enough to toss
from hand to hand? And not a page torn
in fifty years. Before you were born
these little beauties shone on shelves:
Clarity of print, satin feel of paper, rustle of leaves.
Slip one into your pocket.
Read it in bus or train.
Read it in bed.
Read it again.

ILLUSIONS

I thought I heard you calling
As I walked in the town
But when I turned to look I saw
A stranger with a frown

I thought I saw you walking
Just where we used to meet
But when I looked again I saw
A woman of the street.

I thought I smelled your perfume
Elusive and persistent
But when I tracked the wearer down
She was a shop assistant.

I thought your hand had touched me
As I lay in my dreams
But waking from deep sleep I find
Nothing is as it seems.

I thought about the taste of you
So salt, yet sweet to me
But thoughts were only thoughts, alas
Your presence fantasy.

You were not there, you would not come
Not then, not now or ever
Even if I were twice the man
And wise and brave and clever.

THE BALLAD OF KING MIDAS

One early morning for breakfast
King Midas had, so it's said
In a golden cup on a golden plate
A beautiful golden egg.

He picked up his golden egg spoon
And gave it a fearful whack
But the whack with the golden egg spoon
Produced not one golden crack

For the golden egg was rock solid
And gold from centre to shell
So he called for toast and marmalade
But that turned to gold as well.

Each day the king grew thinner
As he gradually faded away
Then he turned to his god Dionysius
And fell on his knees to pray.

He begged for an end to his power
For he knew that he soon must die
So his god sent him for a shower
In the River Pactolus nearby.

And the river slowly restored him
First his feet, then his body, then hands
And the bed of the river forever since
Has been covered with golden sands.

THIRTY-SIX LEFT FEET

This poem should dance and not lumber
This poem should skip in the sky
It should do a waltz or a rumba
But it can't and it doesn't know why.

This poem should play and take chances
Have fun, strut its stuff, have a ball,
But this poem don't know any dances
And it sits by itself near the wall.

This poem once cartwheeled through clover
Where it danced and it sang all the day
But the songs that it sang are now over —
This poem is fading away.

PRUNING

Once I had a poem
full of useless words.
I sent it to a poem doctor
this is what he said:
"Every word must justify
its place upon the page.

Prune and cut:
minimum words,
maximum expression
and no confusing
punctuation!"

Once poem
useless
doctor
said
justify words
prune
maximum expression

I'm so happy.

FOUR-LETTER WORDS

Since I ought to include fuck
at least once in my collections
to show I'm not afraid to use it
let's start this with it. There.
Now to get on with the poem.

I don't give a shit for the word
but it's required, a sort of badge
supposed to indicate a modern poet
uninhibited, liberated.
For up and coming women
it's obligatory, they think.

Words like this are more direct,
incisive, cut the crap.
They used to shock
but usage dulls their impact,
makes one long for words
like wise, sure, love
hope.

POEMS ARE LIKE GLASSES

"Do not stand the glasses on their *rimes*" (English instructions with French tumblers)

Do not stand your poems on their rhymes
It's hard to match the classic paradigms
Any weakness will be found
And your poem will be drowned,
Critics love to punish poets' crimes.

Like a chip upon the round edge of a glass
A bad rhyme is a blemish we can't pass
From the chip a crack will start
And your poem falls apart —
Scrap it, don't be forced to a volte-face.

A cracked glass when you ring it will not chime
And an ill-rhymed poem simply won't keep time
Rhyme well or do without it
There is no doubt about it
You must never stand your poem on its rhyme.

CHACUN A SON GOÛT

If garden snails in plastic pails
Were really good to eat
Would men in bands across our lands
Foreswear the need for meat?

Would garden gnomes in stately homes
Be supervising farms
Of mollusc hosts all climbing posts
And setting off alarms?

And diners go to French bistros
To eat so frequently
When home-cooked fare in open air
was absolutely free?

Or would the taste put pounds on waists
And then begin to pall
And embargo these escargots
From every dining hall?

HOW

How would you handle a tail?
Rub it with ice-cream and spaghetti.

How do you make the sea forget?
Smother it with confetti.

How do you wash your hair?
Drape it over your arm proudly.

How do you nail down a carpenter?
With brass tacks, loudly.

What can you catch on your tongue?
The wild west wind and the raging sea.

How do you unwind a clock?
With spring tides and a left-handed key.

SCIENCE

starts with hope, or even faith
continues with a searching after truth
discovers facts that need interpretation
wrestles with them, seeks illumination
follows false trails, then with some relief
produces theory, a credo of belief
tries and tests it, can't ever be sure
that time will find no fault, belief becoming law.

TECHNOLOGY TRIUMPHS AT LORD'S

Lord's in July. Australia in England – the Ashes.
Unbeaten at Lord's for seventy-five years,
this time they're looking fallible.
Tickets are expensive, rare as wine
in a brewery. Even members are turned away
empty-handed. Queues at the gates
enormous. I take my seat and there's
an empty one beside me as we start.
But not for long.

A man, smartly dressed, perhaps a City type.
Pleasantries exchanged, he reaches in his pocket,
pulls out a sleek black phone, searches for texts.
On it he checks his shares, his diary,
a friend's address, You Tube, the internet,
his fingers sliding screen over coloured screen
like a pianist's.

A bright start by England; runs race
off Strauss's bat and Cook peppers the boundary.

The phone is out again. Curious, I ask if it's
an iPhone and it is. He gives a demonstration:
tunes go in there, the camera's here,
you take a photo thus and look, the compass
finds true North and here's a map of where we are.
A message comes in and he's
checking texts, replying, checking yet again.

Johnson's erratic for the Aussies, Siddle
not much better. Only Hauritz stems the flow.
I turn to share the moment, but he is
deep in texts (phone calls are banned)
receiving, sending, getting the latest prices.

One-twenty-six for none at lunch. What
a morning! We chat again and then he's off
no doubt to banquet in the Harris Garden
or Thomas Lord Suite. After lunch I wait
for his return, but he does not appear
again at all, as England prosper.
So much cricket missed. What a costly
alfresco office. But would I like an iPhone too?
You bet I would.

REFLECTIONS

Light glances off water,
displays broken fragments of the landscape:
a duck and ducklings swimming
rushes on the far bank
the white candles of a chestnut
young lovers walking.

Pick up your camera, fit the polarising filter
look down through prisms and see what lies beneath
the surface. For light is more complex than we think,
has many planes which the camera winnows out
removing distractions, allowing us
to see through appearances
to the underlying truths: the nymph of the dragonfly
impaling tadpoles on its lower lip;
the river lamprey sucking blood
from a fish who cannot shake it off;
the pike lying in wait for the ducklings.

CONSERVATION

We are children of the consumer age
taught to believe growth is essential
which we achieve by a throw-away life-style
forgetting matter cannot be created or destroyed
only changed, a principle well known
to chemists, and dung beetles
who wait patiently for animals to change food
into dung, then pounce upon it eagerly,
roll it away to eat or lay eggs in
for the earth's resources are finite
and so often desirable things
can only be obtained
by changing something else:
earth into metals, trees into wood,
wood into paper, petroleum into plastics
or greenhouse gases, dung into maize,
maize into biofuel into greenhouse gases
which do not hang around to be reused
but float away into the atmosphere
forming an invisible blanket
that will make us sweat.

WONDERS OF THE UNIVERSE

Professor Brian Cox
beguiles us with his good looks
and air of quiet certainty
in the deserts of Namibia.

With a castle and a pile of sand
he simplifies the concept of entropy
predicts the sun's end because
famous thermodynamic laws
decree that all reverts to randomness and disorder
this side of the heavenly border.

What he did not explain was how
in spite of this unvarying law
on a planet of an unstable nuclear star
life could possibly occur.

With destructive forces all around
how could randomness in the end
produce something so well designed
that it goes on and has defied

sun's rays, gamma rays
lashing wind and water waves
fresh water, salt water
immersion deep down under water
seaquakes, earthquakes
ice that covers land and lakes
meteors and quagmires
lightning strikes and forest fires

and all attempts to exterminate some of its forms
and all manner of destruction and harms
changing and evolving through many gestations
of which we are just one of its mutations?

Without some 'Life Force' of its own
could life have happened and have grown?

As likely that monkeys and typewriters, or worse,
could have written all Shakespearean verse.

ASTRONOMY

There is, after all, a point to astronomy,
it's not just a study of astral geography
or a form of optical exploration
or a game of spot-the-comet-conflagration,
not just a search for how it all began
looking for evidence of the Big Bang,
not wild escapism, but philosophy
a direct link to physics and chemistry
a study of creation, a lesson in humility.

STAR TREK TODAY

There's a shop near the station
a placard hangs outside
like an old inn sign
swinging in the wind,
a blue lightning bolt
vivid on yellow
under the word
Teleport.

Inside
I place your photo on the scanner,
in one pass translate it
into electronic impulses
binary sequences
then beam them
with the aid of broadband
half way round the world. There
my contact, Scottie,
guides the signals in,
materialises them
via screen and printer,
and holds your image in his hand.

IN A LIFETIME

IN A LIFETIME

My grandmother was born when the first motor cars
crystallised from Benz and Daimler's minds.
I'm sure she knew nothing but horses
for years, unless the odd bicycle
ventured Norfolk's wilds. Her childhood
was lit by candles, oil and gas,
lacked simple pain-killers, safe anaesthetics,
effective vaccines, antibiotics. The toilet
was a hole in a wooden box out back.

Electricity changed her life at speed
it's hard to grasp: telephones, gramophones,
cinemas, radios and every kind
of home-making machine. The thermionic valve
invented and obsoleted in four decades.

Medicine and chemistry stretched life longer,
took some pain from it.
                                        But the pace:
from pony and trap to supersonic flight;
from peace, through two world wars,
to the nuclear bomb...

*

I open a drawer, at the back
notice my abandoned slide-rule
and instantly know where to look
to try to understand.

I'm back in my youth
when diphtheria, polio and small pox
were feared, remember
leather soles, steam trains, mechanical watches;
hear Lindwall surging in through storms of radio static
to wipe out England's tail in Australia,
replay my first shellac record —

Peter Dawson's "A Batchelor Gay"
from *The Maid of the Mountains* —
spend my weekly shilling on pop
from a bottle with wired-in stopper.

Men have stood on the moon,
had hearts, lungs, kidneys replaced.
Children are conceived in test tubes.
Money is plastic, electronic.
Gay means something else.

And we take these things in our stride
as she did, are thrilled
by brilliant inventions
but seldom grateful,
try modern things as soon as we can,
wonder where it's all leading,
if we can cope with the problems
we're making, get on with life

as she did.

POSTCARD TO FALMOUTH

Picture side, Maidenhead

Punts saunter the river by the sounding arch,
men display in white flannels, striped blazers,
straw boaters; women float by in full white dresses,
mutton sleeves, floral hats. On the far bank, a tea-party
forever goes through hoops on changeless lawns
before a multi-chimneyed mansion. Basking securely
in their leisure, upon this bank a young men's outing
sprawls the water's edge in jackets and cloth caps.

Message side

"Dear Jacquie,
                    I wish it could always be like this
but weather's gloomy here. Paper's full
of news from Austria, some bloke's got shot.
So much I want to say, but I've only got this postcard.
Give my kind regards to your parents –
wish I was home and nearer you, but I must go
on to London. Not sure when we'll meet again.
Yours,   Alan."

Written in the album

"Alan prisoner nr. Salonika, survived war.
Jacquie killed by stray shell nursing at Arras.
How I miss her."

AN ALL-TIME GREAT

On radio, a firm clear voice:
...I worked with Oscar Hammerstein
in 'Rose Marie' - ***and*** *his father...*
Then she must be
very old indeed. More words.
It's Mary Ellis, her hundredth birthday.

I'm listening to a voice first heard
the year Brahms died. Star of The Met
at eighteen, she sang with Chaliapin
and Caruso, went to England
"for love", became Novello's leading lady,
my mother's favourite. I never saw her
but heard her singing
The Dancing Years, Glamorous Night.

An actress too -
Coward, Rattigan, Eugene O'Neill -
last seen acting on TV
aged ninety-five.
Surely she should be living in her past
but life for her is here and now.

Wanting to prolong the interview somehow
I put her record on:

Deep in my heart when the shadows are falling
I hear a voice that is ever recalling...
Magical nights...

TRANSPORTATION, 1945

It folds like a small suitcase,
opens to reveal a serpentine silver tube
grasping a circular head,
a sharp pointed beak of steel,
a felted table centred round
a silver bullet. In the lid
a cranking handle, to be detached
thrust into the box's side
and turned and turned
until it will rotate no more.

Now, out of its brown paper sleeve
you extract a disc:
black, shellac with central label
dog staring into funnel.
Lovingly the disc bites the bullet.
Pulling back the beaky head
you lower it onto the now-rotating
surface, the dog dizzy, the beak
kissing the crackling edge.

And then the miracle.
A tenor turned wandering minstrel,
the Court of Titipu, sailors in topgallants,
a lover sighing and you're transported
to plush seats, low lights, a conductor
twirling his insistent baton, applause,
curtain dissolving into kaleidoscope
of rotating colours, whirling fans
and ritual feet, a wonder world
of unlikely executioners, malevolent maidens,
mad mikados. And then the music stops.

It’s time to pack real suitcases,
sell the magic box, board
an ocean-going prison, set sail
for open seas, perilous passage
and a new world, just as exotic
just as fantastic, uncertain,
but only too real.

THE FLAVOUR ENHANCER

Two young boys roam '49's Ideal Home Exhibition,
searching the everyday for the unusual,
find free samples of monosodium glutamate
wonder 'flavour enhancer' from the USA
lifting chemistry from the classroom into life.

But boys will be boys. Attention diverts
to nearby stand where Johnny Leach,
Britain's new World Champion at Table Tennis,
gives an exhibition of his skill.

And now he challenges young men
to come and taste his power. A brave one
relishes the test, borrows Johnny's bat
so Johnny finds a new one, ordinary
handle, but face a mere two inches
in diameter, like a soup spoon.

Johnny tosses ball, imparts a whirling spin,
difficult to master. The battle's on, white celluloid
flying from side to side at speed,
the challenger angling and smashing
with zest, but again and again
it's drawn to Johnny's 'spoon'
like steel to magnet. The young man's scoring well
against the seasoned master,
returning spin with spice, keeping in touch
till Johnny turns it on and pulls away.
Of course he wins – he is World Champion
and his skill has for sixty years
enhanced at least two memories
of this otherwise forgotten Exhibition.

CHANNEL 4's HISTORY OF LORD'S

A camera roves slowly
black and white terraces
a bobby in uniform
an old man in a mac
the back of a woman
her forties hairstyle
next to her a teenager
who turns towards us.

Is William Boyd right*
that in our lives we change
becoming different people,
our earlier selves
strangers to us now?

The schoolboy turns
looks straight at me
and I know his history
and the woman's beside him
the sharp stab of recognition
cutting away
the intervening years
as if they'd never been.

*In *Any Human Heart*

FINDING THE EDGE

I am always trying to find the edge
but the edge eludes me. If only
I could make the ball an edge-seeking missile
then I would become
the most famous bowler in the world.
Some days it's a problem to make the ball swing,
on others it's not to make it swing too much
or too early. Then there's the pitching of it:
too far back misses the edge, too full
makes the ball easier to hit.

What a difficult art
and a capricious one too,
since it can desert me without warning.
But when the muse is with me,
then how it sings,
song after song, to the most beautiful
timpani accompaniment in the world.

IF WE CAN

If we can find a cause in which to lose ourselves
While we are young
A deep involvement that can so release ourselves
That we belong…

But will we choose the right one and so find ourselves
the space to grow,
Or led by older bad ones won't we see, ourselves
the way to go?

Suppose we won't admit mistakes, deny ourselves
The cause offends,
Would we build mental barriers mountains high, ourselves
And lose good friends?

So is it better to hang back within ourselves
And find our voices
And take our time and learn to understand ourselves
Then make our choices?

Or should we dare do something to surprise ourselves
And risk it's wrong
Trusting, that in the end, we will be wise, ourselves
Becoming strong?

SLUG

what drives you, what drives you
to cross this path of dust
on which the feet of men and sheep
fall like hammers crushing yams?

The odds are fearful. You
moving like a minute hand, so slowly
your shadow lengthens faster,
grit irritating your soft belly
so that you must bind it together as you go
with your own secretions.
And one after the other they come,
uncaring, pounding their huge random feet
on the narrow way.

And do you cross placidly
a fatalist, taking the odds as they come
because they cannot be changed,
neither expecting to complete your journey
nor expecting that you will not,
just travelling because you must,
because the path is there?

Or do you weigh the odds
and still decide
you must go to the other side
driven by some fierce imperative
that makes you dare
now, under the sun's implacable gaze
while the dark birds circle?

SHOPPING LIST

A book of words
Some soothing creams
A box of birds
A jar of dreams

A ray of sun
A crumb of hope
A job well done
Elastic rope

A lifeline smile
Some time and space
An extra mile
A touch of grace

ANNA AT 'IL CHIOSTRO'

1996

I don't know much about her
but she is always there
in the morning with vacuum cleaner,
cheery *buon giorno;* at evening
with plates and food and smiles,
bright eyes scorning the missing language
between us. She makes me feel
I've been given the freedom of the city.
Working so hard, receiving little
to live by save the priceless gift
of joy, she does more for understanding
between nations than all the popes
and politicians in the world.

PLUS CA CHANGE

Before the Euro, 1996

There's a motorway bistro at Spy
From Liege you'll get there if you try
        They've got beef and red wine
        And cheeses divine
But how do you pay when you buy?

Well, it's easy, believe it or not
You can use any money you've got
        You can pay for potatoes
        With Marks or Pesetas
They like Thailand's Baht such a lot.

With French Francs you can go for a pee
For a Pound you can have two or three
        For just a few Yen
        Go again and again
Is there nothing in life that is free?

The cashiers just find it so thrilling
Selling cake for an Austrian Schilling
        If you pay with a Zloty
        It won't drive them potty
You'll find they are ready and willing.

If you give them South African Rands
You will see they just hold out their hands
        And you'll get no kudos
        For cash in Escudos,
They've bundles of Roubles in bands.

But though they take dollars from yanks
One currency earns you no thanks
        When you pay for your fish
        (If you wish for that dish)
Don't offer them nice Belgian Francs!

GOOD FRIDAY IN RELLEU, VALENCIA

9 p.m. Dark, with muted street lamps.
After heavy rain, crowds gather
outside the church, silenced
when huge doors open
releasing gleams of gold
then bearers forming the cortège:
the crucified Christ in gilded glass
Virgin haloed in star-burst rays
on their shoulders. Behind them
mayor and councillors, then the band,
twenty-eight musicians, four abreast.

A drum beat announces departure
establishes the rhythm
which soon becomes a slow, slow march.
Music proclaims the death
of all who've ever died, its mournful notes
bouncing off walls of houses
crowding over the haunting sadness
as band and marchers sway in time:
left— right— left— right as in a trance.

A corner, the procession slows
but never stops playing and swaying
as feet negotiate the turn, then on,
dark marchers joining from doorways
step for step, calm, respectful.

The uncommitted feel compelled to follow,
drawn by the winding tunes,
the swaying rhythm
and something else they can't define:
a language with no words
that speaks to them
and shares the sadness
they didn't know they had.

MARCHING

I tell you, I heard marching
the stamp of feet on tarmac
carried faintly on the black night air
just as the sounds of branch line trains carry
across the valley when the breeze is right,
and a chill crawled across my skin
though it was summer, and I turned to you
for support, but you were sleeping,
so I rose and ran to the window
as if expecting the confirmation of sirens
but there was nothing, except a red glow
over the distant town and the baleful moon
casting a twisted pall of blind shadows
in the orchard. “Come back to bed,”
you said, “it’s all right now”.

I DON'T DO BALLROOM

Do you really want to dance
Or escape while you've a chance
For I cannot keep the beat
There's no rhythm in my feet,
And I know they'll turn to clay
When the band begins to play.
Won't you cross me off your list?
Very well, if you insist.

Am I holding her too tight?
Do I start with left or right?
I can't tell a waltz from tango
Or Castilian fandango.
Is it quick-quick first or slow?
Will my feet know where to go?

I've no rhythm and no rhyme
And my feet are out of time
And my head is in a spin
I don't know which dance I'm in
And the music's getting faster
It's just not a beat I'll master
And we're heading for disaster.

Is it coming to an end?
Am I going round the bend?
I am getting in too deep
Are we're falling in a heap
Could I really be asleep
Or just in SHOCK? *Please STOP*!

DECEMBER

December is the cruellest month
demanding that we all prepare for fun.

No matter if our lives are full of sorrows;
presents, cards must be bought by tomorrow.

Young children help us to cope with what
must be done and for a while shut out

the pain of a dying parent or a sickly grown-up son.
Crueller still, perhaps, for those who've overcome

all problems, are well prepared for wassailing,
look forward to having the family gathering,

the joyous giving, the feast, the laughter,
but death comes in the night and forever after.

Then families and friends are tested
and those bereft must be supported

and funerals arranged and guests invited
and strangers informed and clergymen visited

while the world shuts down for celebration
and long days of happy recreation

and all around the snow lies deepest
and icy winds cut through the weakest.

Should we, at this time, wish each other merry
or prosperous? Or better by far to hope we're healthy

and wiser and happier, rather than wealthy?

LIVING WITH BELLS

Our home's a place where a handbell team
Can learn a tune and practice it,
It's home to us, but also home
To crates and crates of handbell kit.

We've bells in the cupboard
Bells on the stairs
Bells in the spare room
and bells on the chairs

Bells in boxes
Bells in plastic packing
Bells protected
By miles and miles of bubble wrapping

Bells made of metal
Bells made of glass
Bells made of china
And bells made of brass

We've Bluebells
Harebells
Tubular bells
In stair wells.

There's rows of bells by music stands
With handles made of leather,
There's music sheets and rubber bands
That hold them all together,

Bells, books,
Candles for the power cut,
Chimes, at times
And peals from the tower, but

When the team is practising
Although I am no Trappist
It seems that bells are everywhere
And going like the clappers.

There's a bell at the front door
A bell in the hall,
Bells on the kitchen floor
And half way up the wall

There's ringing in the telephone
There's ringing in my ears
There's singing on the gramophone
And bells that no one hears!

But when it come to Christmas time
The bells are out all day
Bringing tunes to folks in rooms
Who want to hear them play

It's then the house is quiet
With spaces everywhere,
It's then I miss the cheer they bring
And cannot wait to hear them ring.

TWO AGING TRIOLETS

1

You speak, but I don't hear
These days I need it twice
The sounds aren't sharp, I fear
You speak but I don't hear.
No matter if you're near
Once will not suffice
You speak but I don't hear
These days I need it twice.

2

I read the words, don't understand
Surely I'm not getting old?
The style is cramped, the words are bland
I read the words, don't understand.
My head's as if it's full of sand
My mind is numb, my blood is cold
I read the words, don't understand
Surely I'm not getting old?

DOUBTS

Now the mark of the leopard is on you
and the Catherine wheel's slowing down
do you feel a sense that you're losing
the will that has driven you on?

Do you, do you?

Have you sensed the hesitation,
is control slowly slipping away,
and do you believe if it's leaving
it will ever return again?

Ever, ever?

When you know for sure that it's going,
and it seems that the best is through
will you keep on, keep on trying
to do what you can still do?

Will you, will you?

Or will you accept that it's ended
that the fire of doing is done
and the moments that make life worth living
are over, all over and gone?

TO MY FRIENDS IN THE NORTH

I love you all, my Scottish friends
I love your loched and mountainous land
I love your tartans and your pride
The sad tales of your history.

But more and more I fear for you
The sense of being wronged that grows
The wish to blame those in the south
For your unease at what you are.

Your history will take its course
And what will be will be,
But never will I love you less
Or you mean less to me.

TO MY CHILDREN

When you are growing old and think of me
And wonder what I'd say if I were near
Take down my books, now you have time to read
And search my words and try to find me there

And if your search gives you some sort of pleasure
I hope amongst my poems that you've found
Some answers to inevitable questions
You wish you'd asked while I was still around.